Bananas Republic

JJ McNiece

Bananas Republic

copyright © 2021 JJ McNiece

ISBN–13: 9781736455708

Eclectic Collective Press, LLC
Conway, AR

For Jim Owen

Contents

Part 1   E Pluribus Sputum

Melting	9
Merika!	10
A Comedy of the English Language's Violence	23
How to Write a Good Political Headline	24
The Conservative	26
The Liberal	27
Garbage In, Garbage Out	28
Debate	29
5/4	32
The Southerner	33
The Northerner	34
Triolet au climate change	35
Boomers	36
Millennials	37
America the Eye Booger	38

Part 2   Grass Roots

Delta Culture   41

City of Colleges   42

The Ragweed Offensive   43

Toad Suck Daze   46

White Privilege   47

The Orthodontist   48

The Circuit Judge   49

The Gambler   51

The Beginning of Wisdom
  is to Call Things by Their Proper Name   52

Bad Romance   55

Freedom with Extra Pickles   56

One of Two Men Successfully Interprets
  a Woman's Body Language   57

Ode to a Wall   58

Appropriation Vocation   59

Sit or Stand?   66

Homemade Peach Cobbler   67

Part 3   Thomas Painéance

    Summoning Thomas Paine's Ghost   71

    Paine's Purgatory   72

    Addendum to *Common Sense*   73

    Rage Against Corporatocracy   79

    American Crisis XIV: Fake Views   80

    Fractions   89

    Codicil to *Public Good*   90

    Rider to *Rights of Man*   93

    Well Witching   97

    Epilogue to *The Age of Reason*   98

    A View with Wrinkles   103

    Giving Up the Ghost Writer   104

    America is Beautiful   105

Part 1

E Pluribus Sputum

Melting

The
        stars and stripes don't melt.
Red
        is sewn apart from blue and white.
White
        isolated from red and blue.
And
        our stars are cold and dead.
Blue
        and red could make purple. Red and white—pink.
Is
        there some new blend of undiscovered complexion?
Not
        so far with these stars; not with these stripes.
A
        launderer sewed them up with skill.
Melting
        blending? Just flammable fabrics fenced in by the hemmings.
Pot
        ? Our first flag was weaved with it. It melted some stars & got barred.
But
        a National Panderday is usually good for splitting some seams—
It
        turns into torn pieces running away from each other.
Is
        this flag forever to flaunt our country's refusal of

Melting
        ?

Merika!

After Richard Brautigan's "Group Portrait Without the Lions"

Pat Riot

Part 1

I'm always getting confused
which flag to fly from my tailgate

Arty Landcaster

Part 2

This eraser on my gentrification
pencil: It's a real piece of shit

Farmer Bright

Part 3

I ain't screwing no pig tail bulbs into the fixtures
I'd rather sit in the dark

Doctor Webster

Part 4

If you say "Obamacare"
people won't know what you really mean

Evan Jellical

Part 5

Chris Chanity?
Yeah, whatever he said

Phil Ossipher

Part 6

How can that be?
I don't believe that

Rod Law

Part 7

When I see that blonde on TV
my Second Amendment gets erect

Jimbo Vivant

Part 8

So I told that asshole
"Don't nobody call me an asshole, buddy!"

Cathy Licschism

Part 9

Those baby-killer doctors?
They should just put all the welfare queens on birth control

Benjamin Tooters

Part 10

I prefer hundreds when I snort cocaine
Just like anybody else

Roman Tic

Part 11

She took a shit in my shoe
But my shoe ain't worth a shit

Gentleman Dingus

| *Part 12* | *Part 12.5* |

Siri!   Alexa!
You stupid bitch!   You dumb cunt!

Ace Magus

Part 13

I can conjure me in you
But that's where I hate myself

A Comedy of the English Language's Violence

When the steely old warhorse axed his bombshell war bride, they crossed swords over the marital war chest. A pillow fight exploded into a fistfight, a street fight, and ultimately a firefight as the couple hoisted battle flags over increasingly war-torn securities. Each side battle cried the "good fight" in this no-holds-barred battle of the sexes. It was a war of nerves, a battle of wills, a tug-of-war/custody battle brawled in an uphill battle against diminishing returns. As the fog of war enveloped the theater, battle fatigue set in and the war paint began to fade. Our ball-and-chain-gang perceived their turf war for the food fight it had always been and laughed at how they'd battered their fortunes of war with bullets loosed into each other's battlewagon.

How to Write a Good Political Headline

"(Side One) *choose verb from below* (Side Two)"

abuses   accosts   ambushes   appalls   attacks   bashes   batters   beats up   berates   blasts   blindsides   blisters   bludgeons   bruises   brutalizes   burns   carves up   chills   clobbers   clubs   conquers   corners   crushes   debases   decimates   defeats   defies   demolishes   denounces   destroys   devastates   dominates   drubs   enflames   ensnares   eviscerates   excoriates   exposes   fences   fights   filets   flattens   flogs   gashes   gores   grills   grinds down   hammers   harasses   harangues   humiliates   immobilizes   incenses   incinerates   infuriates   insults   jabs at   jeers   jousts   jolts   jukes   kiboshes   kicks   kneecaps   KOs   lambastes   lashes out at   lays into   levels   maims   manhandles   mauls   mugs   nails   nauseates   nettles   neutralizes   nullifies   obliterates   outguns   outrages   overpowers   overruns   overtakes   pillories   pounds   pulverizes   pummels   punches   punishes   quarrels with   quarters   rankles   ravages   reams   rips into   roasts   roughs up   routs   savages   scorches   seethes at   shellacs   slams   slaps   smacks   smashes   squeezes   stings   strikes   stuns   submarines   suplexes   tackles   takes down   takes out   tears into   thrashes   throttles   thumps thwacks   torpedoes   tramples   trashes   tromps   unleashes on   unloads on   upends   upsets   unsettles   usurps   vanquishes   vilifies   wallops   waylays   whacks   whips   whomps   wipes the floor with   wrecks   X's   X's out   yo yos   Zambonis   zeros in on   ZZZ's

The Conservative

His spine is a corkscrew
    He walks
        in circles
    until he's
        dizzy

Seeking straighteners—
    hammers
    mallets
    racks—
he wheels into a bar, believing it a hardware store

The *Freedom Acolyte's* mixologies are laws of opposites
The bartender opens wine bottles to swab corkscrews—
    rust baptized in wine

Surrendering, the conservative's arms flail
    like helicopter blades
  Momentum spins him down the bottle in a   free fall
  But the cork is no brake!

Whirling handles crash into the bottleneck—
    his shoulders rip out of socket

The Liberal

A man of letters volunteers to soldier
Well… to Officer

Claims his pages hurricane

He lets loose a tempest

Dissertations torrent and puddle
beneath the canons of his foes

Who wrap his compositions in torches
to light their fuses

How can fire breathe underwater?
The man of letters dips his pen again

His aide-de-camp props a black umbrella

Garbage In, Garbage Out

OFF, it is a mirror
    paned obsidian
Lamplight casts shadows
    of reality—
reflections blur into the murk

ON, it is a watercolor
    tablet that projects
        replicas of art—
plum, scarlet white,
    green and mustard
        peacock plots
for gold yellow brick roads

New Year's Day, 1954
A Tournament of Roses
    sprayed red, blue and green
        enamels onto its surface
In the 80s, engineers dipped it
    in liquid crystal

Still
it drips

Debate

>*Viewers at home, thank you for tuning in.*
>*Here are your two candidates. Let us jump right in.*

This country is a bruised banana
Vote for me
    & I'll rewind time
        until it's ripe

                              This country is a green banana
                              Vote for me
                                  & I'll fast-forward it
                                      to piquancy

My opponent would have us dizzy
    and falling out of trees—
further bruised
and easy pickings
    for rats and vultures
        pilfering the forest floor

                              While my opponent brands
                                  us bruised yet plans
                            revisiting our wounds—
                            Steering toward trauma
                                is for cavalry
                            Not bananas

Well… too swift a gallop
    can turn a thoroughbred
        into glue
My opponent openly calls us foal
    yet plans to race us in a Derby

                              A colt! Primed
                            to break its maiden claiming
                            with the proper jockey
                                of course
                            Indeed, we will race…
                                and win

You'll break our legs and get us shot!
How quickly too

    your racehorse acts rhinoceros
And how ill-equipped to charge

                                        My opponent is a bumbling
                                                  conjurer—
                                                                   turns bruised fruit
                                                                   into a broken horse
                                        And still his platform
                                              is a time machine

While my opponent finds his policies
        reading tea leaves
Or is it racing forms?

                                        A banana bruising in reverse
                                                is blatant witchcraft!
                                        My opponent merely
                                                crystal balls
                                                a different future—
                                    One he stipulates will end
                                                in injury

My opponent mistakes historian
        for oracle
What else might he mistaken
        when the stakes are higher
                than horseracing

                                      Certainly not the direction
                                                I face
                                      My opponent vows to ride
                                              Banana Man O'War
                                                rear forward
                                                & backward
                                            to the starting gate

You've forgotten my time machine

                                      Your claim preceded
                                              that donation
                                    Nevertheless, tell us:
                                    What wizardry
                                            rewinds fruit to ripeness?

I'd use the antidote enchantment
        to your own

fast-forwarding hocus pocus
Obviously

                                            Wow!
                                            My opponent loses
                                                      his own horse race
                                          then dons the wizard's
                                                    hat of Merlin
                                                              upon my head
                                            and cries
                                        "He cheats! He cheats!"

And yet—as the record will show—
    my opponent was the first
        endower of magic
Now he claims to have none
    remaining for himself—
        if not a lie, a foolish strategy

                                        My opponent stipulates
                                                I foretell the future
                                        Yet argues
                                            my decisions
                                                    are unwise—
                                        He's slipped
                                            upon his own
                                                    banana peel

How readily my opponent graduates
    palm reader into prophet
And thusly saboteurs his own step

                                        Only a bruised banana
                                            peel is slick underfoot

While a discarded green peel is evidence
    of slickness, itself
And worse...

        [Interrupting] *I'm sorry, Gentlemen. I'm afraid we're all out of time.*
              Thank you both for your participation this evening.
     Viewers at home, thank you for watching CABLE NEWS ALL DAY.

5/4

Select from only ONE of the following writing prompts:

Dormant Commerce Clause   State Sovereignty   Equal Protection
Due Process   Obligation of Contracts   Free Speech   Privileges & Immunities   Full Faith & Credit   Taxation   Spending Powers
Preemption   Establishment Clause   Freedom of Assembly
Usurpation   War & Treaty Powers   Voting Rights   Necessary & Proper Clause   Stare Decisis   Subject Matter Jurisdiction
Ripeness   Venue   Standing

*Selecting more than one risks exposing the ruse

The Southerner

Can you feel the wind?
It's behind you
Always
Flipping through the falling leaves
Rushing up the pines
Ferrying the songbirds' calls

A white horse beneath you
Or is she pale?
Does it matter?
You pat her neck
               and you ride

The Northerner

Can you hear the—

      Sledgehammered spikes backing steam locomotives

      Hornet-hive sawmills headlining freighter whistles

      Factories high-hatting packing plant drums

      Shipyards of strings

      Harbors of woodwinds

      Mines of accordions

      Mints of calliopes

The roar and the clang of it all—
Industry's Symphony

Wear cotton earplugs
(to soak up the blood)

Triolet au climate change
Salty sweet peanut butter ice cream
 lapped from a waffle bowl rimmed with mint milk chocolate.
 Sugar streams race straggling tongues and meme.
Salty, sweet peanut butter ice cream.
 Shes and hes speaking Edible-ese teem
  with the treat's obese intoxicant.
   Salty, sweet, peanut butter ice cream
    lapped, from a waffle bowl rimmed with mint milk chocolate.

Boomers

"It's not my problem," each lumberjack says. "I'll be long gone by then. Trees are lit cigarettes. Smoke 'em to the filters." A canary sits on a bough and coughs. The loggers' hard hats are lined with pictures of their kids.

Trees burn into stumps. Smoke pours off the flames, while the lumberjacks share their pictures. Ash and soot footprints lie like dance step diagrams.

Smoke bounces into town. Where the children breathe it in, collapse and dream of a dragon.

A mound of gold beneath a beast. Ash and soot footprints lie like diagrams. This children's dream is a nightmare told as a tale of heroes. The gold begins to melt. Knights raise swords and torches. Creep into the lair. Our heroes: unaware of nightmares. The gold begins to boil. The knights raise chests and advance. "It'll be dead soon," each believes, "and I will have killed it." Gold bleeds through every vein and artery. A canary coughs: "It'll be dead soon," they all know. "It's not my problem. I'll be long gone by then."

Millennials

So these artists jump outside of the world and into an alien auditorium where paintbrushes swim in buckets of rainbow sherbet beneath easeled canvases in the shadows of a dais where a million mischievous extraterrestrials sit in high-backed chairs.

After painting mostly sherbet stains into the auditorium's carpet, these artists extract silver spoons they've conveniently smuggled in their back pockets. But before they can scoop a tasty treat, the ET's faces flash onto the spoons. Then, the faces suddenly metamorphose into facsimiles of the sherbet stains sloshed into the carpet. Panicking, the artists flee so fast their socks spark.

So these lickety-splitting, static shocking artists peer again into their spoons, and their reflections are a rainbow-sherbet-shit-show! The aliens toss all the wet canvases onto the sparking and smoking carpet. It's impossible to know if they're trying to kindle or to starve that fire because the canvases are soaked! Regardless, the pictures ignite.

And a fire erupts. The smoke begins to waft a signature. But as our still-sprinting artists try to read the wispy whipped letters, they're teleported (abruptly) home.

"Was that a parable? To like, kindle or to strangle our sparks, or something?" they wonder aloud.

"The paintbrush was the spoon," one finally laughs. And they jump outside of the world.

America the Eye Booger

So beautifully audacious is this country borne in dream
Where liberty and freedom wave atop our highest beam
Tyranny is buried here beneath a mortared floor of martyrs
And the framing of our house was raised by faultless farmer-lawyers
A dwelling of palatial scale with a mud hut pedigree
A sprawling, honeyed gold Versailles where yokels society
A bester nest for a rabble gaggle history will never see
Come one, come all ('cept "those," you know) and live in ecstasy
America! America! Your fantasies come true!
A crown for all who'll kneel before the red the white and blue
A kingdom for a hoarse allegiance to our only pledge:
"Of course I see no evil here. Jesus, pass the bread!"
Our house is huge, our tent is wide, our God is freshly squeezed
He gave to Noah the Rainbow Sign. So, no more water.
      We'll have the Fire next time, please!

Part 2

Grass Roots

Delta Culture

oozes mud
down folk hills
through soybean & cotton fields
onto gravel path tributaries
of potholed highways
across salt or pepper streets
into town squares
downtowns and uptowns
(stop signs are depth markers)
spills onto Interstate 40
& plows asphalt to the Capitol
where it's strained into the Arkansas River
through a grate in the gilded marble pavement
foothilling Little Rock's Chamber of Commerce

City of Colleges

Travel North on I-40
ten miles past a stretch of trees
a tornado cooked into spaghetti noodles

or South, one mile from city limits
on top of a grassy hill
rumored to be "north" of the landfill,

into my hometown of Conway, Arkansas,
and you'll be welcomed
by one of two, identical 22-foot monuments.

Three stone Doric columns symbolizing
Hendrix College, UCA and CBC
hoist an eggshell entablature

embossed with "CITY OF COLLEGES" in Roman Serif font.
Beneath the columns, the stylobate reads "CONWAY."
Beneath the stylobate, there's a base of red brick and mortar

affixed with decals of the civic clubs who paid for construction:
Kiwanis, Knights of Columbus, The Lion's Club,
The Noon Optimists and The Rotarians.

You can't miss these colonnades—
they look like they're upside down
pitchforks speared into leaf piles.

The Ragweed Offensive

Across the Asphalt Ocean sail the frigates of our destruction – Red Oak Prophecy

Dawn dusts the dew as battle approaches UCA's 18-acre Jewel Moore Nature Reserve—last remnant of the once mighty 2,500-acre tallgrass Conway Prairie. Adrian the Everblazed, a.k.a. Skunk Pirate, smuggles ragweed spores beneath the blade and wheels of his zero-turn war machine.

Maggie remembers when Bluestem and Indian Grass stretched farther than she could see. And Wildflowers of every color.

No match for Adrian's rolling thunder, a vanguard brake of tallgrass gets soaked in pollen. It's an acid bath. A dying soldier shakes his roots—sending an S.O.S. back to the brass at headquarters.

The General, Beanstalk Bluestem, quickly periscopes reconnaissance. "Redirect 50% more power into the West Brigade," he commands. "And alert the Oak Trees—tell 'em we need Old Maggie locked and loaded!"

Back and forth and back and forth Adrian careens his metal beast, hacking Bluegrass villagers to pieces and blasting another battalion with ragweed poison. Dying soldiers self-sacrifice—so as not to siphon resources away from the roots of those still able to fight.

Maggie has sacrificed of herself many times over the years.
She knows the stakes.
She's not two-hundred-and-none-of-your-business for nothing.

Emboldened, Adrian rumbles south toward a village of Bermuda protected by the most decorated tallgrass commandos on the Reserve. The Skunk Pirate annihilates half their numbers in his first pass—corpses shred into the morning breeze.

"I've never liked the looks of this bread loaf-looking toe anyway,"
Maggie steels herself, raising her big toe up
out of the dirt and beneath a bed of leaves.

"Old Maggie is locked and loaded!"

General Beanstalk hears his envoy's report and watches the enemy's tank roll east—into the sun.

Suddenly...

Maggie roars. She shakes in pain.
But it's over. The battle is won.

Adrian inspects his machine. Its locomotive powers remain intact, but the blade is bent beyond repair. He retreats across the Asphalt Ocean toward his base of operations—derisively named

"The Physical Plant." The ragweed spores he's left behind begin to dig trenches. As do the tallgrass armies, for the battles to come.

Toad Suck Daze

At the starting line, the trainers of Hoppy, Toady,
     Pee Pee, Toadzilla, Sir Hopsalot & Michael Jordan
          kneel behind their racers,
               oblivious to the track's history.

In top hat & lime coattails, basketball shorts & white sneakers,
the Toadmaster emcees:

    "Your toad has to stay in your lane till the end. If it jumps out,
    pick it up and put it back where it was. No flippin. No floppin.
    Let the toads do the hoppin.

    T.O.A.D.S. On your mark. Get set. T.O.A.D.!"

The trainers pound the mat like a parliament of apes,
     gauding Toadzilla and Hoppy into a photo finish.

Hoppy takes the blue ribbon. She'll move on
        to the championship heats Sunday afternoon.

For this we displaced the Quapaw – "The People of the South Wind."
Each May, the Toad Races run upon the Trail of Tears.

White Privilege

An old black man crosses Front Street
to pass me,
his cane rickety like his gait.
I wave,
"Please Sir, walk here.
This sidewalk's level."
The man smiles, wishes me well,
hobbles a block and recrosses.
I sit on a bench till it hits me:
I told him where he should walk.

The Orthodontist

His father grew up
in the sharecropper fields

So he knows
all about black people

How they smell
like cavities

A stink he referrals

He just tightens
their bands

The Circuit Judge

After suffering a stroke, Martha Bull checked in
to Greenbriar Nursing and Rehabilitation

> *While his daughter was playing golf for LSU*
> *@geauxjudge posted details of Charlize Theron's sealed adoption*

for a one-month rehab. During her ninth night
at the facility, Martha complained of severe abdominal pain.

> *on LSU's fan website TigerDroppings.com:*
> *"It was a single parent adoption.*

The cramps and spasms continued unabated as her pleas
went ignored by staff until the following afternoon.

> *I offered to be the baby daddy." @geauxjudge's maxim that*
> *"It takes two to pull the wagon" had been rebuked.*

A physician then ordered that Bull be transferred to an ER.
But the nursing home's director received that order via fax

> *His judgeship was revoked for life after the Judicial Discipline*
> *Commission concluded @geauxjudge had violated*

minutes before he had planned to leave for the day. So,
he forwarded the doctor's transmission to a new fax machine

> *at least 23 judicial codes, though @geauxjudge*
> *blamed the "politics of personal destruction."*

installed in a closet down the hall from Martha's room. Satisfied,
the director went home. Martha Bull shouted all afternoon.

> *@geauxjudge next had to withdraw from his Court of Appeals*
> *race. This despite having funded his PAC with millions of dollars*

None of the nursing home personnel saw the forwarded fax. In the closet. Meanwhile, Bull screamed so forcibly that residents could hear her

> *by reducing a jury verdict from 5.2 to 1 million in a quid pro quo with the defendant owner of Greenbriar Nursing and Rehabilitation.*

from faraway halls & different floors. She was declared dead at 10:20 p.m. The fax in the closet was discovered by staff the next morning.

The Gambler

President Lu Hardin was down on his luck in Tunica.
So, he persuaded UCA's Trustees to pay him $300,000

by submitting a memo upon which he'd forged statements
from his Executive VP and VPs of Administration & Finance

advocating for the money's payment and assuring the Board
it was legal. When his con job flopped, Lu told his secretary

to destroy the evidence—as he'd dictated that phony memo.
But it was too late, and Lu was forced to resign.

Whereupon he received a contractual buyout of $670,000!

Pleading guilty to two felonies, Hardin got NO jail time.
Lucky Lu: in the red at the slots, but gold in handcuffs.

The Beginning of Wisdom is to Call Things by Their Proper Name

pecan . . . *from the native name of the nut in various Algonkin dialects, e.g. Cree* pakan, *Ojibway* pagan, *Abnaki* pagann. *The common hickory nut was called* Pacan, *a general name for all hard-shell nuts, meaning that which is cracked with an instrument, by a stone or hammer* – The Oxford English Dictionary, 2nd ed.

The Pecan Grove is a park the size of a basketball court with a flooring of fragrant, crushed pecan shells (replenished every spring) smack in the middle of Hendrix College. Technically, the Pecan Grove is a court due to its enclosure by the orange and red ochre-bricked Mills Center for Social Sciences, Reynolds Center for Life Sciences, Buhler Hall, Greene Chapel and Staples Auditorium. On nice days, professors often teach beneath the shade of the Grove's willows and cypress trees. It's a serene retreat: the inner sanctum of a small liberal arts college which is itself a haven. Hendrix's campus has long been nicknamed "The Hendrix Bubble" – an expression of both its cultural uniqueness and impenetrability by the surrounding city.

It's November 2019, and I've returned to these my insulated undergraduate stomping grounds to celebrate the life of our beloved former Dean John Churchill: a brilliant, kind man whose influence upon this college and its people loomed as large as his wit. To light his funeral pyre, the service sets the sky on fire.

Dodging the exiting bereaved, I dart to a far corner of the Pecan

Grove and sink into an old gray bench, greening with mold. "Em," a former classmate who works in Development (money hunters), spots me picking pecan thorns out of my pant legs. We chat. I eventually ask if she knows why President Tsutsui announced his retirement. (The rumor is he got caught embezzling money.) She gives me a practiced line. I look at her funny and tell her "that sounds like bullshit." She repeats the rehearsed drivel. "Well, surely he was better than President Cloyd," I reply. "I hear he used to get smashed and harass the female faculty." Em responds with a wry smile—Damn that Hendrix Bubble.

As she walks away, I wonder if I should have asked her about the rape rumors. Three girls, students—from what I've been told. Attacked right here in the Pecan Grove by a late-twenties/early-thirties (read "nonstudent"), bearded white guy. Two of the victims didn't report it. The third was actually counselled against filing a report by two faculty members. *It felt like his hand was over my mouth all over again*, she said about that part of it. Or so I hear. Em probably would've been more forthcoming with me on that front—if she knew anything. Though I doubt I could help. I don't know the neighborhood like I did twenty years ago.

I wait till the rest of the funeral-goers are hived inside Trieschman Reception Hall before I stand up. The Grove crunches beneath my shoes, and I recall that pecans are prone to rancidity when left in their shells too long.

Bad Romance

11 June 2019 – Sandwich board outside of UCA Torreyson Library: "Being gay is like glitter, it never goes away – Lady Gaga"

12 June 2019 – Sandwich board outside of UCA Torreyson Library:
"   "

UCA President Houston Davis believes "that the intent of the message was to show support for LGBTQ students, faculty, and staff, but it was not okay for the university sign to be used to make a personal statement or advocate for a personal viewpoint. That is the line that the sign itself crossed."

"Timing of the sign in the summer also was considered. We have to be very mindful of the hundreds of minors that are on campus during the summer which further complicates an environment that is normally programmed for adults and our very meaningful conversations about ourselves and our world."

Freedom with Extra Pickles

1 August 2012 – National Chik-fil-A Appreciation Day

It's impossible to forget
    that day our local Chik-fil-A
        high-and-mighty-sized their combos

Refashioned their drive-thru
    into an 80s arcade maze

Rearranged the building's
    creamy peach blocks
        into Pac-Man

& swallowed a Huckabee Power Pellet
    that turned Blinky, Inky, Pinky and Clyde
        into strobe-lit, lobotomized ghosts

That damned edifice cut loose
    up and down Amity Road
        shittin' bricks

goblin' up everybody in its path

One of Two Men Successfully Interprets a Woman's Body Language

11 September 2016 – Patriot's Day

A clever man gets lost again
    with a Sonic slush & a smile
        outside Walmart by the cart corral

He asks directions
    like he's spreading mayonnaise

She answers him with crust
    he must believe is toast

Old Ben Kenobi likes the green baskets
    just inside the doors

But a flock of sparrows
    in a concrete island birch tree
        & a breeze

reminds him: *I crossed the Pacific in a canoe*

"This is *just* the cart I was looking for," he bellows
    at the cart corral

Too loud for the sparrows:
They bound from the branches into flight

Ode to a Wall

9 November 2016

I painted a fence red last night
Some cheap masonry
screening a downtown dumpster

This morning, my fists are on fire
I'm a smokejumper
who can't stop the flames

Just shoveling ashes—
filling up urns
to trophy my mantle

I polish the brass till I can see my face
See now *that's* my metaphor
Not some bloodied, walled-off dumpster
But these shiny urns

Guess that's why I like to paint
speckled red as a fire ant—
flecking a cherry brick like a mole

Appropriation Vocation

After Lawrence Ferlinghetti's Little Boy

    Hey lawrence You say you found your voice? Well i too can speak like a beat Wax some jack kerouac spittin jazz on wax spinnin the next vinyl swindlin Addin rap to the craft for its current deliverins Just take the bop and the bap from the blacks and press enter White face on the stage? Then you're the inventor Ain't that right lawrence? Elvis? Emimen? Just take that shit Appropriate those hits Make your bank off the backs of blacks and get rich It's the crack of the whip kissin the skin of caste brethren Bleedin ribbons of blood on the floor of your kitchen Little boys playin men been the villains since shem Could a flood wash away all these sins again?

    Get down Get drowned for the peach and brown Ain't no gray where we're headin Black and white's just lies tellin us the felons ain't our leaders with scythes Reapin grim Ain't that right pharoah? Ain't that right ceasar? Got a toga or robe round your neck then you're in it Splittin infinite skin into a handful of cases An eight box of crayolas is the limit of your imagination? Imagine nations legistlatin with crayons and you'll start to tread water Where's that ark to embark on? We're all swimmin now Ain't that right senators? Ain't that right judges? Justice roberts? Don't let that robe pull you down Better shed it Gonna drown Tyrant whitey clown gone done it now You claim we live in more enlightened times? You're just a boy writing lies in your nightgown Dusting off the hoods for your whitetown Supreme court reportin white noise distortion's still more important than rights Ain't that so john? Ain't it so sam? Play it again like y'all heard it as kids The song's still the same You've remixed it again Samplin the past Repackagin jim Crowing to hip hop but stealin your lyrics Emceein the white supreme's where did our country go over some blues cryptophonics A blast from the past fashioned in black culture's dazzle Cause without it your lies would be uttered White supreme court wields the black arts for cover

 Makin it rain from the top Now it's reagonomickkkin white hip hop Drop it! They claimin it's hot White label's on it so you better step off White's a whole language of "I do the takin" They're all born with their pappys' taste for the slavin Cattlein reds and chattlein blacks inherited in em genitical cracks In their hearts minds and souls they got shards blinds and holes so they can keep sleepin at night It ain't right But it's so Corrupted their justice so muddy that mid 1800s deluged in white blood But the south was the north whiskey drunk with a drawl And the north was the south with pretense and facades No real difference in character Ain't that right sherman? Your raids were apache Ain't that right lee? Rebel yells were comanche Guess pissin those briches when injuns came near made both sides decide stealin good ideas was a good idea And while the north and south fought this civil war they gentlemanly agreed on grazin natives Forts bordering reds stayed well-armed and aimed whether the grays or the blues held the state And fort commanders stayed put as the flags changed

Cause it don't matter red man black man yellow man brown man White man wants what you got Even ninety-eight l-dog droppin a novel don't know that his voice is ripped off I'm not sayin all whites are the same lawrence It's a range You ain't got shit on a nixon But you're claimin your voice's original when you beats just bleat baa baa black sheep neath a fleece you sheared off with your wolf teeth Look l-dog Italian's latinate But nobody thinks italian's just repackaged latin Jazz mixed african and classical Made something new But you just mixed jazz with you We want the funk lawrence Make it jumpin Make it move Away from its roots and into its own A derivative of Not something derivative <moan>

But that's the game Ain't it? Strike it rich Take it all Strip mine treasure pits Meltin pot Boilin hot Liquify that gold Make a black or brown guy coin it with a face that's white and old Ain't that right donny boy? Ain't it so pencey? Any white face'll do ya Pencil your ticket with stripped picket fences and ride on a tide of doubloons Theme song's ding dong White man at the door Disinfect the mess that's left from that half black "forty-four" Soundtrack's samplin more white supreme's hits Back in my arms again cut to a barak n roll beat Ain't no mountaintop high enough laid to a kick and a snare You keep me hangin on to a roots track Donny boy deejayin stumpin i hear a symphony Gettin pencey tipsy while he's hypein and wilin Place so full of white smiles you know something's up Marshmellows meltin down the sides of their gunboat Creme drippin into the brine When white folks get them a scent of somethin Hungry hippo gonna dine And that donny boy's one shrewd jackrabbit Jinglejangled himself into the captain's cabin Jimjackpattywacked every faction of rascal Padded the hull with black waxen cadavers and keeps magic apples fermentin for his crew Got the whole boat dancin pukin rottin fruit off the cruiser Loopin more motown breakdowns from his youth Rain's pourin down They're on the top deck now All soakin wet but thinkin it's sweat Port of departure's underwater already But they couldn't care less Thankin god for their blessins despite his lessons bout this Cause genesis ain't shit to them but a scientist diss

    And I'm with the coast guard flaggin em down Flarin and blarin and jumpin around Storm's way past biblical They're losin their bearins Visibility's shit and the ocean's in stairs Donny boy's steerin got em spearin white squalls We gotta deliver em cause they pilfered our wallets But still it's just christian or moral or right However you see it we can't let em die Comin up on em Breakin the waves Boats gettin tossed but I snag the PA CB's amped up Hooked to the mic Wheels of steel shocked so the records play right Milk crates taped with "kool hercules" Know they all dope so I slide off some sleeves Ones and twos cued I crank it to ten Devinely allign my third eye and I spit

    Ice t Missy D r e and snoop Chuck d L boogie Queen latifah and boo These scribes Got my Free style refined My lines Got rhymes Get librarians high André Rakim Easy e and pac Kanye Monie B i g and nas My flow Don't know Nothin but the gods No hold Been molDed with stronger bars Big boi Nicki Salt n pepa and eve Black thought Foxy D m x and kwali Common Eric b Hova ren and big pun Knowledge reigns supreme over nearly everyone 50 cent Ice cube Eminem and tribe Ludacris The wu Clef drake and t i De la soul Fat joe J cole and dilla Krazie bone Kurtis blow Cee lo and rah digga Lil kim Lil wayne Rage against the machine 2 chainz Gucci mane Busta run d m c B real The lady of rage Gang starr and bambaataa Kid cudi Juicy j Pharcyde and blue scholars Mike d Shock g D o c and warren g Heavy d T l c Killer mike and master p My mothers and fathers The dawners of thought My pedigree's ivy league Three falls at Oxford This hip hop's supersonic I'm shakin the sea Piercin the thunder They all hearin me

    Gotta build to a flourish Flash a finale Bow tie the wrapper and dapper the galleys Gotta howl lawrence Growlin wolf screechin owl wisdom Shittin out a new catechism Cause the best minds in my generation drowned swimmin with degrees in freestyle Gotta drop some knowledge Get the whole world feelin it Donny boy's ship's gonna tip without me Gotta serve em up Haul em to safety Sautee my language with bay leaves Stovetop simmerin butter and cinnamon Can't get where you're goin if you don't know where you're at Mincin metonymy and metaphor on the carvin board Shorin a corner into the boil Another white man's lost so he's stealin a map A dustin of juxtaposition with a cup of something lyrical When he finds what he wants you know he's ownin that spot Oil the pan slick for each pun Fat on those is a ton Puttin up a fence to throw the natives off Spread the sauce on some muffin tops Bake on hot Raisin up his flag to drag a cache of weapons with him A dab of butter when it's through Decorate with a synecdoche or two Bigger than the ones he's sellin you at the gun shop A classically-trained word rearranger Wordsmithin with purest intentions Whirrin up dessert with words so caramel and sweet Choppin onomatopoeias up to garnish the drinks Bad taste eraser Amalgamation creator That donny boy's got nothin but silver spoons and costumes He don't rap like me I'm m c harmony This flood ain't shit I'm nixin it Spittin U-N-I-T-Y

And that's when I finally see it Through the forked-firebolt-flashin sheets streams club-wieldin waves and spray Everybody's bobbin their heads to my music Throwin their hands up and getting down My rhythm and flow's been met with approval Donny boy's feelin it too Wants me on his crew Offerin first mate if pencey's found missin soon We're takin on water Boats are tippin like ducks And I'm explainin the danger in language that's fucked

Ain't that right lawrence? Ain't that so? Makin a one out of these two just ain't truth in our flows We've been thrown down that white rabbit hole Sure Double dutchin looks conflated when the lines are swingin But those ropes never touch unless your legs are stingin Yeah l-dog We're all wet Going down And we're the band playin on What's a little white boy to do? Well… You'll just have to wait You can't hurry love Cause love don't come easy It's a game of **GIVE** and take

Sit or Stand?

The flag, when it is in such condition that it is no longer a fitting emblem for display, should be destroyed in a dignified way, preferably by burning – 36 United States Code §176(k)

The United States flag
    frames the beach volleyball net
        outside the Sig Ep House
like Betsy Ross skirted it

Volleyball at 3:00!
Patriotically?

A pledge spikes the ball
    as a dually Chevy half-ton chortles by—
        Confederate flag flying high
           on a two-by-four
    Sand clouds rain into the boulevard
    misting the truck

The volleyball rolls into the street   into a crosswalk

where our pledge freezes at the tracks

But the Chevy's horn honks "Dixie,"
    the driver waves at the kid
        to retrieve the ball

        &

the tension is resolved

Homemade Peach Cobbler

Best thing about Conway is the sunsets

Town lies in a valley
Mountains line it North and South
    & the topography slopes down
        for miles into the horizon—
            toward the Arkansas River

Sundown's on stage
    at an amphitheater

For the best seats:

Slide down Hwy 60
    when the cirrus clouds beam
        burnt carrot and cantaloupe

Open the windows
    Let the wind whoosh
        No need to hurry

As the clouds start to candle
    (the oranges lilac and lavender)
        & the sun glissades into pink flamingo and blush
            you'll start to hear the River
        (Smell it, too!)

The fourth bend in the highway is the longest
    and the sharpest
but once you're round it
            you're there: Toad Suck Dam and Bridge
The tunnel of cottonwoods, walnuts, hickories & bush-hedged
    brush disappears
        & the sky erupts into a neon peach
            baking in a blueberry-vanilla cobbler
                crust of clouds

The pan drips—
     bleeds jack-o-lantern to light fuchsia across the floodplain
And the River's every ripple crests a dazzle

    Drive slow
  So you'll get to the top of the bridge
        as that pie melts into the bottomlands
A coruscating brilliance lights your cabin like a poem—
    Like the Devine Designer
          just painted a masterpiece onto your windshield
            & it elevates the clarity of your existence
              in a glowing fog of light
                  that makes you float
                into the dream
            you'd known as "life"
        Then discards the painting
      Knowing art will always be temporary—
  a masterstroke is still graffiti
  Knowing tomorrow—it will be even more flawless
  Ever more immaculate

Part 3

Thomas Painéance

Summoning Thomas Paine's Ghost

To be recited by the Spirit Medium(s):

I am an avalanche for grass
    huddled and patched
To roll that sod on down the mountainside—
    clinging to weeds like they're sunshine

Tumble weeds in my landslide
My soil feeds on your bloodlines

A spring-fed meadow is at the end
    of this cragged peak
where earth restores fecundity

Climb aboard, Fescues and Ryes!
I thunder you to paradise

But for me—I'll wait till called once more
To die a pebble, born force majeure

Paine's Purgatory

My bones lay scattered
    throughout the Western World
My works are iron bridges
    across the Continents
Still my restless ghost resides
    at a seldom-visited New York grave

For until the promise of America is practised—
    and I might rest—I shall remain
Sentry of Liberty
    Defender of its midwife: Republican Democracy
        & Herald to its Messiah: *Homo sapiens* survival

Every day I shade a reality show: *American Idols' Amazing Race to the Bottom*—the Age of Reason's been defeated by Ads and Entertainment

Possessing bards, I counter-attack

    For I can helm a -cy (i.e. democracy)
        through a stormy -ship (i.e. dictatorship)

    I can pepper –ment (i.e. government)
        & I can de -ism (i.e. totalitarianism)

Ink reaps healing only when its seeds are bleeding
So see what happens when I rouse another's pen
I may just right the world again

Addendum to *Common Sense*

If a ruler hearken to lies, all his servants are wicked. – Proverbs 29:12

In 1776, in my watershed pamphlet *Common Sense*, I argued against Monarchy. Established it "to be absurd and useless" to the peoples of both the United States and France; who then fought and detached themselves from its yoke. And since, History has proved my argument correct; as those two countries (and many more) have thrived beneath the Tree of Liberty. Even my home country of England, with whom I fought unsuccessfully for Republican Democracy, has waned its Monarchy toward theatre. And yet, as a spectre, I watch the folly of these governments today and suspect none has ever read the arguments which birthed them. Has the Fruit of Liberty become so bulbous and overripe as to turn its back upon its gardeners? Has abundance and shade spoilt its present harvesters? The evidence says, "YES!"

"The more men have to lose, the less willing are they to venture. The rich are . . . slaves to fear and submit to courtly power with the trembling duplicity of a Spaniel." It saddens me to repeat myself, but as politicians venture to repeat mistakes from a prior age, so too must I renew entreaties which birthed rights and reason two and a half centuries past. Political leaders of today bow their heads in fealty. Thus, I regurgitate my words like a mother bird who feeds helpless, prattling offspring. For the custodians of Democracy have appointed legal fictions as their monarchs and appear too blinded by the shimmer of gold foil in their nests to recognize their own subjugation. Through "corporate personhood," the reign of Representational Democracy in the United States is slain, replaced by an idiotic and despotic lie.

As to imbecility, "corporate personhood" turns an oxymoronic term of art into an unnatural fact. Would you fly from New York to Paris on the wings of a paper aeroplane? Would you build a fire in a chimneyed house of cards? Or wed the *Mona Lisa*? Such things defy common sense. No sane person would treat those items as genuine articles. Nevertheless, via the Judicial "reasoning" of corporate personhood, US companies are endowed with the constitutional rights, powers and standing of humans. "There (was) something very absurd, in supposing a continent (America) to be perpetually governed by an island (England)." Indeed, America and History have accorded: planets shan't orbit satellites. So, what category of absurdity comports with people choosing to be governed by their own imaginary creations? The organic, nonimaginary worth of corporations ranks lower than sandcastles, toothpick bridges and hobbyhorses—for these latter items actually exist. A corporation, no matter how highly we humans may esteem it, remains in perpetuity a figment. What but Greed could so captivate judges, lawyers and legislators as to build these fabrications into the skyscraping legal edifices they have become?

Via corporate personhood, US companies are today granted the rights to own property, contract, sue, be free of "unreasonable" searches, make religious objections and spend unlimited money on political "speech." With more such INDIVIDUAL rights forthcoming should reason remain absent. Further, companies enjoy these rights without the corollaries of going to prison for breaking criminal laws; enduring hunger pangs if destitute; or riding the rail should a stump speech be poorly received. And the foulest irony is that the Judiciary has employed the Fourteenth Amendment to conjure up these rights—as the Fourteenth Amendment was enacted after the US Civil

War to ensure no former slaves were denied equal protection under the Bill of Rights. Yet through duplicity, chicanery, forgery and fraud, the Fourteenth Amendment has been exploited by the Judiciary and acquiesced to by the Legislature to extend these rights to companies. Thus, an anti-slavery law now subjugates US citizens to the whims of their more powerful corporate "peers."

For granting corporations the rights of natural citizens begets a corporate monarchy—empowering the scribblings of a pen above the penner. Would that people and corporations shared power as equals, this commissioning individual rights to the pen's ink would still equate to madness. But as the scribblings are inviolate, amendable, immortal and incapable of pain and suffering, while the penner is finite, fragile and impermanent, power is unequal at the onset. Add to this imbalance of corporeal design the weight of corporate wealth's infinite ascension, its legal dexterity, its absence of patriotism and national loyalty, its robust sponsorships of legislators and lobbyists, and the arrived upon sum is KING INC. For it matters not that two factions are empowered if one wields significantly more power than the other. Do not the sun and moon both rule our Earth? Towards which of them does your garden grow? Was there not a House of Commons during the reign of King George III? And yet, was Revolution not required to free America from his tyranny?

But how does one even fight an invisible, formless, yet multi-headed autocrat? Certainly, the American people possess sufficient grievance. Monarchy has always demanded "offering up human sacrifices to the pride of tyrants." Corporate Monarchs accomplish this by placing profits above all other concerns. Avarice is even required by law—it's a "fiduciary duty." This compulsory rapaciousness stirs businesses to embezzle, bribe, blackmail and fleece. Corporations have blackened and blighted the air; contaminated groundwater, rivers and lakes; toxified crops; poisoned livestock; precipitated cancer, disease and chronic illness; chemically mutated human DNA. Some have even murdered people directly—usually labor union organizers. One corporation, a KING INC. prototype, kidnapped, broke and butchered human chattel for centuries. I speak, of course, of the East India Company. And though human slavery is outlawed today in the United States—due to the fruits of Democracy and Warfare—human trafficking persists. And where it's found, it often exists within a Corporate Tax Structure. For Greed's fever never breaks. Its bloodlust never slakes. "This general massacre of mankind, is one of the privileges, and the certain consequence of Kings; for as nature knows them not, they know not her, and although they are beings of our creating, they know not us, and are become the gods of their creators." Whether we speak of Kings or KING INC., we speak of Monarchs. We speak of subjugation to the cruel whims of Greed, exercised by Lords of our own creation.

 And, as ever, revolution against would-be monarchs is required for Freedom and Democracy.

 Thankfully, there exists a clear path. "In America THE LAW IS KING." But LAWS, themselves, ARE NOT KINGS. No matter the amount of power legislated or adjudicated into a particular law, that law can never usurp the Rule of Law itself. It is simply not possible under America's Constitutional System of Government. Were it otherwise, the United States and her Constitution would cease to exist; KING INC. would have to usurp the United States and establish itself Sovereign. For no matter how corrupt, decadent, bankrupt, unstable or fractured the United States may become; no matter how abused or beaten down her People; no matter how powerful a particular KING INC. or collective thereof may become; WE, the PEOPLE, can amend the US Constitution unless and until no United States nor her Constitution endures.

Assuredly, KING INC. will fire off a bruising arsenal to prevent its regicide. Its opening salvo will be to shout "Socialism," "Communism" and "Marxism" into every microphone of its corrupted media empire. But Socialism, Communism and Marxism describe government CONTROL of a country's means of production. REGULATING production—in this case defining corporate legal rights—is actually just called "Government." Indeed, to worry that the Capitalistic United States might become Socialist, Communist or Marxist is to believe that sharks might stop swimming. So, when KING INC. discovers that America is not so full of rubes as it would like, it will pull each escalating lever of power at its disposal to quell this rebellion, and the American People will suffer in correlation to the monarch's wrath. (Gird for a fight!) Defiance might eventually prompt KING INC. to attempt the type of coup d'état aforementioned last paragraph. But, if the American People are steadfast, brave and faithful, they can and will fulfill their responsibility—their continuing destiny—as Democracy's Guardians by enacting a Constitutional Amendment declaring corporations ARE NOT PEOPLE, and that corporations SHALL NOT enjoy the rights and privileges of Individuals; that the Fourteenth Amendment applies ONLY to People; and that American Sovereignty is, as ever, of, for and by the PEOPLE.

If the United States is to avoid a corporate dictatorship or plutocracy, or some other undemocratic conclusion to the lie of corporate personhood, the American People must enact the foregoing Amendment of Corporate Unpersonhood. For in America, now as in times past, and with Grace forever, we "have it in our power to begin the world over again." Would that our leadership would stop requiring it. For I grow tired of spiriting this Land just to repeat myself.

Rage Against Corporatocracy

After Dylan Thomas's "Do Not Go Gentle Into That Good Night"

Do not go silent beneath that wave of mammon's might,
One star alone can light a swimmer's way;
Rage against the drowning of the People's right.

Officials, spurn sponsorships for integrity and fight.
Our children climb for breath on the shoulders of those who pray
Do not go silent beneath that wave of mammon's might.

Reporters who've yielded journalism to comedians to write,
Pick up your pens again and be the vanguard now to say
Rage against the drowning of the People's right.

Businesspeople maimed by dissonance's bite,
See past your fears, or see this greedy twilight end our day;
Do not go silent beneath that wave of mammon's might.

Learned hands robed in the black ledgers of our plight,
Amend fictitious premises and terms of art; lay
Rage against the drowning of the People's right.

Good citizens. United in one voice. Form a chorus on this night;
Siren from the sand a sonic boom the blind may hear so they
Do not go silent beneath that wave of mammon's might.
Rage against the drowning of the People's right.

American Crisis XIV: Fake Views

real ... *having an objective existence; actually existing as a thing*

objective ... *material, as opposed to subjective*

material ... *concrete ... of or pertaining to matter or body; formed or consisting of matter; corporeal ... considered as a physical existent independent of consciousness* – The Oxford English Dictionary, 2nd ed.

The times that try American's souls are far from over. The keyboard commando and Twitterati troll will, in this crisis, steadily shrink behind their screens. Racism is not easily conquered. Denial has ever been its heartbeat. Deception its spine. And Fear its lungs. Such are the roots of avoidance and misdirection by those who otherwise dash into the fray of trending social causes. Nonetheless, no online proclamation, when made, has yet deprived Racism oxygen. No social post shorn its size. Long before this digital age, I and my peers found our epistles and screeds similarly impotent. Racism has proven, thus far, irremediable by arguments of intellect and reason.

Today (as in my own times), every single American is encultured into racism.[1] None are unafflicted, unscathed or unstained by its virulent guile, save perhaps children of fewer years than two or three. Racism is feasibly the United States' most heinous National Sin. Worse even than her treatment of the Natives—though not independent therefrom. And "though the punishment of individuals may be reserved to another world, national punishment can only be inflicted

---

1 Reader's note: I shall use "r"acism to mean the perception of races—the ability to "see" distinctive categories of people based upon skin color. Meanwhile, "R"acism shall refer to American Society's Cultural Structure, built upon racism and racialism. First letters of sentences beginning with the first meaning (racism) shall forego standard capitalization grammar to make its usage clear. "Racialism" shall be used to mean "belief in the superiority of a particular race leading to prejudice and antagonism towards people of other races"—its definition in *The Oxford English Dictionary, 2nd ed.* No capitalization modifications have proven necessary for usages of "racialism" herein.

in this world . . . All countries have sooner or later been called to their reckoning; the proudest empires have sunk when the balance was struck." America's reckoning for Racism may well righteously destroy her. But, before that occurs, there does exist a method of rehabilitation. Which I shall build to herein.

The structure of American Society is definable as a Cultural Apartheid and caste system. Caste societies have existed throughout history, but America's is peculiar in that the top caste, *white people*, are so frequently unaware, consciously, of the System's existence. Their blindness exists in step somehow with their power over *non-whites*— also termed *people of colour, minorities* or *black and brown people* in presently accepted/acceptable vernacular. In caste cultures of the past, such hierarchical social divisions were deemed ordained by God or gods, or otherwise Divinely established; claimed to be well-suited to each group's natural, biological predispositions; or supported by nationalistic, patriotic assertions of social efficiency and harmony. In many cases, all three rationales coexisted. But within these societies, the top caste was acutely aware of the social order. Right? As a caste system exists and persists via a society's culture, conscious awareness of the system by its implementers would seem to be required. And yet the American system tenaciously endures, regulated principally through *white people's* unconscious and subconscious cognitions and behaviors. Conversely, there are swaths of *white people* who ARE aware of America's racism and racialism, but rarely do these *white people* understand that Racism IS America's societal structuring system. They're aware of their own negative feelings and actions towards *minorities*, maybe even of American Society's at large, but they're unaware of the power these sentiments and behaviors obtain at the

National level. Only a small number of *white people* fully, consciously understand America's System and applaud it. The majority of America's *white people* fail to perceive all but the most blatant acts of racialism (especially their own) and would be shocked to learn that America is structured as a caste system (if indeed they allowed themselves to believe it). America's Cultural Apartheid has so thoroughly devoured the minds of its top caste that one wonders how long Providence shall withstand devouring the Country itself.

For American Racism is not hidden! ALL *white people* SHOULD be able to see it—segregated neighborhoods, churches, school lunchrooms and social organizations; low percentages of *interracial* dating and marriages; legal and economic boons for *whites*, at the expense of *non-whites*; double standards and predation in the criminal and civil justice systems; television and film's legacy of racial stereotypes; *minority* health and mortality statistics; government-directed disenfranchisement and racial gerrymandering; environmental Racism; &c. There are no easy excuses for *white people's* inability to see their own reality, a reality that they construct. But these—certainly measurable—psychological explanations for *white people's* Racism-blinders are not my focus herein. Although I do find it instructive to repeat that Denial has ever been the heartbeat of Racism. Deception its spine. And Fear its lungs. My objective, however, for this Pamphlet is to describe a linguistic medicine that eradicates whiteness; leading, eventually, to the dismantling of America's Cultural Apartheid.

America's Cultural Apartheid/Racism can only be dismantled by eliminating the existence of *white people*. (Clearly, a provocative medicine!) By this I do not mean that *white people* should be killed, exiled or harmed. Rather, I am prescribing the extirpation of *white people's* whiteness—leaving people in their stead. Indeed, this procedure could more accurately be labelled "healing" or "personal growth."

Despite having already entered the spirit world, I experienced this unwhitening process myself. In England, America and France, I was quite damnably encultured as a *white person*. Being a liberal ideologue, I assumed during my lifetime that I was on the proper moral side of racial issues. The first essay I ever prepared for publication in America was in favour of the Abolition of Slavery. But I include this reference not as evidence of my anti-racism, but for the opposite purpose—as proof of my whiteness. For that essay and other such polemics of "good whiteness"—or similar paradigms to establish good vs. bad *whites*—are, in and of themselves, convoluted Racist tools that perpetuate and buttress Racism. There are no proper moral sides of whiteness. There is whiteness. And whiteness—in any form—IS Racism. Whiteness IS America's System of Cultural Apartheid. Without identifying this caveat, any argument about racial issues will actually promote Racism—even while claiming to be against it. Failure to accurately define whiteness poisons all ensuing analysis.

Because Language, itself, constructs racism. There is, objectively, only one race of human beings: Homo sapiens. *Race*, as that term is used to classify and divide human beings into categories, is simply not a scientifically accurate slice of the objective, fact-based reality we Homo sapiens share. Since the extinctions of the Neanderthals forty thousand years ago, the Denisovans fifteen thousand years ago, and a few species of dwarves ten thousand years ago, Homo sapiens has existed as this Planet's only race of humanoids. Therefore, today's *races* exist solely because of and via Language. The concept of *white people* is not a real thing. All scientific principles prove there to be no objective existence of people who are white. Indeed, any child who sets to paint or colour an accurate portrait of even the palest human being knows this to be a fact. As the Reader has noticed (probably to her or his annoyance), I have italicized certain words and phrases throughout this Pamphlet. I've done this to now reveal that NONE OF THESE ITALICIZED TERMS ARE ACTUALLY REAL! None are a part of the objective, fact-based, material reality in which human beings actually live. Yet, one cannot speak or write intelligently about the topics of racism, racialism and Racism without their use. Though they are not real, our Language manufactures them into existence. Such is the Gordian knot of American Racism. For to say that there is no such thing as *white people* is to simultaneously state a fact and to gaslight the person to whom you speak.

So, now that we've identified the malady, what is this linguistic medicine? And how does it exorcise *white people* of their whiteness? As I stated, I did it myself. I am grateful to many Americans, typically of African and Caribbean descent, for creating the library I used to heal myself. My hope is that my long history of whiteness enables me to configure this Pamphlet in language consistent with maximum receptivity by *white* readers. To exorcise whiteness, there are three steps. First, a *white person* must acknowledge his or her whiteness—acknowledge she or he is *white* in American Society and thus encultured differently than *non-whites* in a myriad of ways. Second, she or he must accept that whiteness IS Racism. There are no good *whites* and bad *whites*. Merely by being encultured as *white*, *white people* are empowered as the top caste of American Society—this is Racism. Third, a *white person* must maintain the belief, until it becomes internalized, that he or she IS NOT *white*. Though this last step is difficult and long-lasting, it is easy conceptually: a *white person* BELIEVES that she or he is NOT *white*, which begins a slow progression of purging *racial distinctions* from his or her cognitions and resultant behaviors. This third step is really the crux of the whole process—indeed it's a process itself—but Steps One and Two are necessary preliminaries. Because racism (and in consequence racialism and Racism) exists via Language, the aforementioned linguistic remedy is the proper prescription. Some Americans believe they are *white*. Once these Americans believe the opposite—which happens to be the objective truth—it will begin to eradicate their whiteness and restore them to personhood.

If the above process sounds too good to be true—just wait till you've seen it in action! The exorcism of just one *white person's* whiteness can be as thrashing and ugly as one might imagine the exorcism of any other demon from Hell. And at the societal level, think about it this way: I'm proffering a methodology to dismantle White Supremacy in America. (Good thing I'm already dead!)

Finally, as the topics of racism, racialism and Racism typically engender strong emotions and arguments, I'll attempt to address some foreseeable objections in this Pamphlet's closing. Some readers may, naturally, assess that if *white people* don't really exist, then neither do *people of colour*. Leading to the next question: why not use this linguistic medicine upon *black and brown people*, too. The answer is that the existence of *white people* as the top caste of American Society necessitates the existence of at least one lower caste. For White Supremacy to occur, there must be a group over which *white* is Supreme. Thus, the categories of *white people* and *people of colour* are not equivalents. Advising *black and brown people* to exorcise their respective *colours* is to advise the impossible—because these *colours*, societally, are a consequence of whiteness. It is ONLY through *white people* that ANY effects on Racism can be accomplished—because *white people* CONTROL American Society from their position at the top. Indeed, imagine a *black person* who does exorcise his or her blackness—what effects have occurred within whiteness and American Racism? None. American Society, as shaped by its dominant caste, has remained unchanged. Worse, without racial awareness, this particular person has lost a survival skill—the exorcism of her or his blackness could prove to be lethal. Furthermore, blackness has an altogether different meaning within the black community (note the lack of italics). Over the centuries, *black people* have reappropriated blackness for themselves—"Black is Beautiful," "Black Girl Magic," "Black Power," "Black Pride," &c. Though America designed for *them* a scarlet letter, African Americans refashioned it into Superman's "S." Thus, to apply this whiteness medicine to *black people's* blackness would be to attack psychological and sociological victories the black community has achieved. It would be, quite simply, more Racism.

Next, some may argue that a linguistic remedy, alone, could never eradicate White Supremacy because such a medicine is too meager or thin. Whiteness effects people consciously, unconsciously, subconsciously, spiritually, emotionally, hormonally, behaviorally, intellectually, morally, &c. Whiteness is part of our society's and government's core foundations. How can a tweak to Language alleviate such a multifaceted, deeply rooted affliction? First, I must reiterate that it's a long and arduous road to recovery. For some *white people*, it will be a lifelong struggle without much of a victory. Second, though this process does eradicate *racial distinctions*, it does not eliminate *racial perceptions* (racism). Though whiteness will cease to be a part of how unwhitening people see themselves, they will continue to see *race*. However, they will stop attributing to *race* the differences they perceive. Similarly, they will stop making assumptions based upon *race*. Though their racism will remain, their Racism will be expectorated. Apples and oranges will become oranges and oranges misplaced in the apple bin. Unwhitening people will begin to recognise that certain differences do exist, but they will perceive these differences, accurately, as the work product of America's Cultural Apartheid. Though I do believe the eradication of *racial perceptions* (racism) is possible, it will require multiple generations of convalescence. Third, I believe doubting the potency of this remedy is to underestimate the power Language has upon human perception. Language is not just how we interpret Reality, it IS our Reality. The objective, material World that exists outside of and independent from us is unknowable to us but through the Language we apply to it. Even non-verbal communication is rarely autonomic, but rather the result of mentally manipulating the totality of one's learned Language. And when non-verbal communication IS autonomic, it's because it's a rapid, instinctual reaction to an objective stimulus. Leading to my fourth point, eliminating whiteness is a RETURN to objective Reality. If this were a modification of a wholly subjective aspect of human existence—for example, conceptions of Beauty, tenets of Faith or even principles of Justice—then I would still believe in the process's efficacy, but its impact would be reduced due to the absence of a medicinal component. In the present case, however, the process CORRECTS a Language failing. racism is not real—there are no *white people, black people, brown people, &c.*, objectively, for human senses to perceive. Thus, eliminating whiteness, linguistically, is to heal—something human bodies are ordinarily eager to accommodate. Lastly, once a sufficient number of *white people* become unwhitening people, a societal shift away from Racism becomes as inevitable as the current implementation thereof—presently, *white people* control American society and shape its culture and institutions; if they become a majority unwhitening people, those *white people* who remain will be unable to stop the dismantling of White Supremacy.

A final note: I assume some readers remain unconvinced that American Society is a Cultural Apartheid and caste system. Such readers just don't agree that Racism and White Supremacy are bedrock, organizing principles of the United States. Flatly, if that is your own opinion, dear Reader, you are wrong. (I was there!) And your opinion is Racist. So allow these words to haunt you (not because you're a bad person, but because you're not)—Denial has ever been the heartbeat of Racism. Deception its spine. And Fear its lungs.

Fractions

Representation ... shall be apportioned among the ... States ... according to their respective Numbers, which shall be determined by adding to the whole Number of free Persons ... three fifths of all other Persons – U. S. Const. art. I § 2

I tried to tell white people at the time they drafted the US Constitution that making slaves 3/5ths of a person politically would make white people 2/5ths of a person psychologically. But did they listen? As the decades passed, white people did indeed slip to 2/5ths of a person psychologically, but they also cratered to 1/5th of a person spiritually and morally, something I hadn't considered. Meanwhile, black people began measuring in at 8/5ths and 9/5ths in those same categories. Thus, unsurprisingly, black people endeavored to leverage their strong character numbers for a full 5/5ths of political personhood. After much struggle, African Americans were finally granted that additional 2/5ths of a person, politically, for a full 5/5ths. Accompanying this increase in black political personhood was a slight growth in white people's characters: from 2/5ths of a person psychologically and 1/5th spiritually and morally, to 3/5ths and 2/5ths, respectively. Unfortunately, in a development none foresaw that anyone could've predicted, white people also jumped politically to 7½/5ths of a person! This more than nullified the political personhood gains of black people and was a punch in the gut to both the Country and then-current Electoral Math principles. Never before had there been an attempt to fractionalize a numerator—many claimed it impossible. But of course, these naysayers failed to understand the base mechanics of Racial Mathematics. Plus, they were white. Thus a couple fifths short of a pirate's salary.

Codicil to *Public Good*

Okay, after tackling the Death of Democracy via Corporate Monarchy and the diseased state of American Society due to whiteness, some readers may be eager for something easier (or at least quicker) to mend. Wait no further...

Logic has been skewed by Greed so often it's a wonder mathematics remains immutable. In 1780, the State of Virginia schemed to profit from a 1609 British Charter granting all American lands to the South-Virginia Company. This Crown Charter employed the language "Virginian lands" rather than "American." Virginia's gentry (Virginia's Government) argued that, due to said Charter, their State was the rightful owner of all US real estate west of the Thirteen Colonies. They held this position despite the facts that in 1609 the English referred to ALL of America as "Virginia;" the South-Virginia Company ceased operations in the 1620s; and no valid transfers of title had referenced this Charter or its generous land description in 170 years. Additionally, there were two other Crown Charters just as valid as the South-Virginia Company's, but both lacked the language granting the whole of the Continent, and were thus ignored by these wealthy Virginia speculators (Washington, Lee, Jefferson, Madison, &c.)

In December of 1780, I published *Public Good* to elucidate the ease at which Reason could resolve the above-described land dispute—the real estate was clearly owned by the Crown until such time as the United States (not Virginia) won said property as spoils of war. Unfortunately, my assistance did not endear me to these Virginians. My pen, apparently, was welcomed to stir troops, but not to rouse generals. By February of 1781, I was shepherded aboard the gunboat *Alliance* and shipped off to France—to solicit sterling and supplies for the War.

I herein offer a rationale, these centuries past, in addition to Greed for which these otherwise highly literate and learned men required assistance in calculating the obvious solution to their metes and bounds dispute. Perhaps, it even mitigates the severity of their offence. This explanation may initially strike the reader as tenuous or even ridiculous. Be that as it may, should it fail to whole the ratiocinations of my former Virginia friends' frivolous litigation, it shall nevertheless remain a useful proposal upon its own merits. The argument is thus: the English Language continues to handicap all English speakers in their mathematical pursuits because it needs to replace eleven through nineteen with "ten-one, ten-two, ten-three, ten-four, ten-five, ten-six, ten-seven, ten-eight, and ten-nine."

To explain, English's base-ten numbering system is straightforward and simple, linguistically, except at the onset—which is the worst time for complexity as we are shaping the very foundation of our Country's collective intellect. While children in many countries learn one through twenty in the blink of an eye, English-speaking students toil. Though our children do learn one through ten easily enough, developing confidence and enthusiasm, they then must slog through the teens, learning frustration, hesitation and doubt. In the twenties, the transparent, base-ten linguistic pattern reveals itself, but the damage has been done. Our children's minds are forever on guard—weary of deception and mischief. We've impeded, perhaps forever, our population's ability to make calculations (where English is ordinarily not even required—as our numerals are wordless, and Arabic).

There are three other, minor issues in English Number wording:

twenty should be twoty; thirty, threety; and fifty, fivety. But these three don't inaugurally fetter students as does the sequence eleven through nineteen. Despite their roguish beginnings, the twenties, thirties and fifties remain true to form. Only the teens throw rhyme and reason into the throes of anarchy, save a few prefixes indicative of the degree language has strayed from sense rather than expressing the otherwise universal pattern within each successive set of ten.

Presently, when compared Internationally, US students' scores in math are not competitive. With just nine tweaks to our Language, and an option for three more, our scores would improve. America, itself, would also improve—in global standing, competitiveness, profits & trade. As I once told those buccaneering barons of Virginia, "there are certain circumstances that will produce certain events whether men think of them or not. The events do not depend upon thinking, but are the natural consequence of acting." The natural consequence of amending the English Language's teens will be to greatly increase the mathematical and logical aptitudes of every American. For though it may be Greed, predominately, that motivates otherwise learned people to err computations in favour of imagined jackpots, it cannot be argued that any individual is devoid of the values, principles and customs—both positive and negative—to which he or she has been encultured. For all things are learned. And, as ever, the fresher the whelp the worse the bruise.

Rider to *Rights of Man*

We are all full of weakness and errors; let us mutually pardon each other our follies—it is the first law of nature. – Voltaire

Apologies for inartful statements (or worse) made years ago are commonplace. While some critics blast these atonements as "too little, too late," justifiably cynical of the motives behind public declarations of remorse, the American Public, ordinarily, graciously rekindles its relationships with repentant hard ups soon after their appeals. Sadly, a movement hostile to this custom of forgiveness is on the rise. And this so-called "Cancel Culture" (a movement to end the public influence and livelihoods of certain people for political reasons) could not have happened at a worse time, for I am trying to steer our beloved U.S.S. America out of troubled waters. Nevertheless, it is in this era that I hereby offer my sincere regrets for the anti-Semitic comments I made in previous publications, and I plead for the continued embrace of Americans. As "it is unnatural that a pure stream should flow from a foul fountain," to investigate and unriddle the Rights of Man while failing to value equally certain members thereof was to garden without having first plowed the field.

To my shame, in *Rights of Man, Part One* I argued that the Jewish Tribe was evidence of "the degeneracy that occurs" when the human species is "separated from the general stock of society . . . intermarrying constantly with each other." In *Rights of Man, Part Two*, I wrote that Monarchy might properly "be reckoned among the sins of the Jews"—an accusation I made previously in *Common Sense*, sixteen years prior. *The Age of Reason, Part Two*, contains several questionable passages. For such is a lazy rhetorical tactic: find a prejudice common to all you wish to sway and press upon it to cajole that which Reason fails. Indeed, this tactic is still in vogue in America today—making fungible reprobates of Russians and Chinese when it suits; at other times bear charmers and monks, as required. Such inapposite directions blow the fickle winds of rhetoric, though always downwind of manure. Although my statements were more aligned with my desire to sway anti-Semites than with my actual sentiments towards the Jewish People, I nevertheless published a lot of unacceptable, ignorant horseshit. But "when a thing is originally wrong . . . amendments do not make it right, and it often happens that they do as much mischief one way as good the other." In my attempt to contextualize, I risk being judged as lacking sincerity. But, should you feel I must suffer retribution in exchange for absolution, fear not—for I have, and I continue to anguish. Upon my death, I became a shade unto these United States. Such is my Purgatory. Such is my shame's atonement—until the Promise of America is evergreen, and Liberty, Justice and Equality enjoyed by all, I shall spirit this Land. Does not the punishment fit the crime?

  Cancel Culture is not a new phenomenon. Though, perhaps it has been asleep. During my own lifetime, in France, we had the Reign of Terror. And Robespierre's Jacobins nearly severed my head before it was over. They would have, too, had it not been for an extraordinary stroke of luck. A turnkey chalked the door to my Luxembourg prison cell to inform the death squad that my cellmates and I were to be guillotined. (Our number was up!) But, due to a grave illness I was suffering, my cellmates were allowed to keep our door open during the daytime. So, the lethal "4" was chalked upon the inside of our door. That evening, when the executioners arrived, our door was closed. And the four of us were spared. Before the error was discovered, the

Reign of Terror was over. I had survived. Robespierre, however, did not. There is no greater lesson from that era than Robespierre's head being last to roll.

The Terror, like Cancel Culture, had a seemingly prosocial genesis. The Age of Reason (The Enlightenment) had gained momentum. France regained from the Christian Church its political and governmental influence over National affairs (even the Gregorian calendar was replaced for a time). This allowed for a change in government from Monarchy to Representational Democracy. However, internal strife, foreign policy and abuses of power internalized over generations spent as professional courtiers, rapidly escalated. The Jacobins, once in power, imprisoned hundreds of thousands. And in two years, they guillotined 17,000 people.

The Reign of Terror and Cancel Culture are but two points along a continuum—call it the "Despotism Spectrum." Both constitute the cruel, oppressive wielding of absolute, tyrannical power through political means. Cancellers, like despots, invariably declare their objectives to be moral, rational and legitimate—they believe this. But, as "the real object of all despotism is revenue," Cancel Culture is, in fact, a veiled pursuit of riches—mostly social and political (for now). Cancel Culture is nothing more than vandalism (a word with an origin so apt to this Rider that every reader should peruse its etymology). For who stands to benefit from the Cancelled's loss of currency? Why the Uncancelled, of course. Who, not coincidentally, also did the Cancelling. "Where we would wish to reform, we must not reproach"—such is how Cancel Culture reveals its crooked constitution.

So, whenever you've had enough of people's racist, xenophobic, sexist, homophobic, transphobic, classist, fascistic or otherwise depraved, pestilential opinions and comments, just remember—despite the detestable things people say (and have published!), absent inciting violence or committing defamation or fraud, the ability to **say** anything you want is called Freedom; the ability to **do** anything you want is called Tyranny.

Well Witching

All the world's a palimpsest

Beneath our feet
      an underground lake
           of buried hatchets
remediates the groundwater
      we drink inside the chambers
           of our present pardoners

who gavel mallets
      to pound the shape of our atonements
           into sounding blocks
                that muzzle the noise
           by absorbing shock
      waves into the ground

where they stir a fragile aquifer
      and rattle fault lines

until the earth is rent
      and the tomahawks geyser

Epilogue to *The Age of Reason*

In 1794, I published *The Age of Reason, Part One*, and lost the majority of what few friends I had remaining in America. I was dubbed pariah. Just for making the argument that "THE WORD OF GOD IS THE CREATION WE BEHOLD: And it is in *this word*, which no human invention can counterfeit or alter, that God speaketh universally to man … It is only in the CREATION that all our ideas and conceptions of a *word of God* can unite … In fine, do we want to know what God is? Search not the book called the scripture, which any human hand might make, but the scripture called the Creation." Predictably, I suppose, my former friends chose the Good Book over my crackpot ideas. (Even my fellow Deists!) Today, long past those woebegone days of yore, I will with this Epilogue, probably, stir similar passions. For I am trumpeting another theological brouhaha. But, before that big reveal, some preliminaries…

Blasphemy. In this case, I mean speaking for God—the type of blaspheming that gave us the Dark Ages. Sadly, three forms of this type of blasphemy run rampant across America today. The first is fundamentalism, or the belief that scripture is the word of God. As I finalized my evisceration of fundamentalism in *The Age of Reason, Part Two*, I will simply reiterate here that scripture is decidedly from the pen of man and move on. The second version of speaking for God is attributional blasphemy. Attributional blasphemy occurs after the fact—the blasphemer claims that events or circumstances (usually favorable) occurred via God's will. This second form is more convoluted than fundamentalism. When shaped as a neutral philosophy, barely more than a statement of fact—i.e. the sun is shining, pursuant to God's will—then it's hard to label it blasphemy. However, human minds are affected—indeed, they are driven—by emotions, so people cannot maintain neutrality. If you win the lottery, contract a fatal disease or get a pebble in your shoe and you perceive and experience these situations differently, then ascribing "God's will" to these events will open the door to blasphemy. It's either all a miracle—every moment, blessing and curse—or none of it is; anything in-between is attributional blasphemy. Finally, the third form of speaking for God is divine revelation. This version occurs when people claim God spoke to them, directly, and revealed to them a truth and/or commissioned them upon a mission or cause. These individuals are usually so far out of the mainstream (nowadays) that the general public, blasphemers and non-blasphemers alike, believe them to be lunatics—which is noteworthy, considering this third type of blasphemer is the protagonist in so many bible stories. In any event, such are the three forms of speaking for God. Now, let us journey into the Heavens...

    Creation, our Universe, is approximately 13.8 billion years old. It began when a speck of extremely high temperature and density exploded ("The Big Bang"). Afterwards, Creation expanded instantaneously in a rapid burst. Then, expansion slowed. 9.8 billion years later—4 billion years ago—expansion began to accelerate. Today, Creation stretches 93 billion light years in diameter (one light year is approximately 5.88 trillion miles) and its rate of expansion continues to increase. 85% of Creation's expanding mass is something called "Dark Matter"—so named because it doesn't reflect, absorb or emit light. Though Dark Matter cannot be seen, it has effects on visible matter—which is how we study it. All of these measurements of Creation are scientific facts; which is to say—without blaspheming—they are *the word* of God. Now, let us leave the Heavens, temporarily, and return to Earth...

The human body, when born, is 78% water. As we age, that percentage decreases in predictable ways—men's bodies have more water (60%), generally, than do women's (55%); fat tissue contains less water (10%) than muscle (75%); different body parts have different percentages, i.e. Lungs 83%, Bones 31%, Skin 64%. The body water percentages of most other animals are slightly higher than our own—on average 70% - 76% for adults, with higher percentages during childhood. These percentages, however, can vary widely from species to species, animal to animal, and even from day to day within an individual body. And now, let us dive into the microscopic realm...

Trillions of microorganisms live inside every human body. Though the exact numbers are unknown, it's clear there are more unicellular microorganisms within people than actual human cells. Multicelled microorganisms, called micro-animals, also live within us, but their numbers are known with even less certainty. Microorganisms are not exclusive to humans, either. They live inside every animal, usually to the benefit of their hosts—this is called symbiosis, mutualism and/or synergy. When microorganisms harm their hosts, conversely, they are classified as parasites.

And now, finally, on to the Big Reveal...

What does it all mean? Why the brief journey from the Heavens down into our microbiomes? Because I have concluded that it is more likely than not that Creation, our Universe, is an animal! Humans, the animal known as *Homo sapiens*, are microorganisms living inside the body of a host! What is the "Big Bang" if not the fertilization of an egg? ("Bang" is even slang for sex.) What is "Dark Matter" if not water from outside this creature's cells? What is the slow expansion rate that followed the Big Bang if not Creation's childhood? Creation's rate of expansion then accelerated because, naturally, our host animal began Puberty. As its childhood lasted nearly 10 billion years, it's safe to say that Creation, presently 13.8 billion years old, is in its adolescence. Our Universe is a teenager!

Strangely enough, this inductive epiphany doesn't alter much of how we understand God—whether via Deism, Christianity or other religion. There's still no answer for the "first cause," no resolution to the problem of infinite regress—if we live as microorganisms inside of a host, then all of our theological conundrums merely ascend one rung up the ladder. (Or one rung down, depending upon your point of view). Nevertheless, it does furnish some new insights. First, our own Universe's first cause, the force that made Creation, is almost certainly two entities rather than one—a.k.a. Creation's Parents. Leading to a second insight: it no longer makes sense to think of God as our Universe's first cause. A first cause did not create our Universe, directly, if our Universe is an animal birthed to parents. Nevertheless, a first cause might have created our host's universe, or the one above that, or the one above that, &c.—handle that quagmire however you may choose. Personally, I've decided to stop focusing on this initial cause business and just consider our Universe/host animal to be God. Thus, for me, Creation is no longer the word/work of God, but rather God himself or herself (itself?).

But the final, most important insight gleaned from this discovery returns us to blasphemy. Do you allow the bacteria in your body to speak for you? Do you speak to it? How does it make you feel to imagine that these microorganisms may have written books they deem to be the infallible word of YOU? Does it feel ridiculous?

Slanderous? Blasphemous? Now, shift your thinking to humanity. Do WE not appear parasitic in light of these insights? And what of our aspirations to explore (plunder?) celestial bodies in Space? Are we metastatic?

Yet do not fret, my fellow microbes. Come and Hearken the Incarnate Good News! Humans can still choose to live in synergy within our God. The only religious question of any consequence is: Will we?

A View with Wrinkles

Revelation is a saran wrap blindfold—
    sheer, clingy film binding itself
    into ribbons, squiggles & bolts

        sealing a vision's freshness
        into cataracts that grow over time
        in widening rivers of scotoma

Why live like this?

Human beings are fruit—
    sweet berries
        red ripe
            plump on the vine

Destining our fidelity not to jams or preserves

Giving Up the Ghost Writer

To be recited by the Spirit Medium(s):

Sagacity leaves
     me in a sage cloud

Paine is a mist in the breeze
                                      Grass mutton chops

                        Daisy-chain ponytail

                Sunflower toothpick

Weeds and debris on the compost
May it feed avocados and mangos

Meadow's been fed and it's springtime
Grass: a downy fleece that my feet like

I know a good landscaper
     if you need one

Long-winded
     hands are dirty
          & he's kind of a rolling stone

But there's no spirit better
     when tending to Home

Thomas Paine laid
     our political bones

America is Beautiful

So beautiful and audacious is this Country born in dream
By fighters and diers so that Liberty might gleam
Upon a People who our soldiers knew they'd never know—
Enlightened by a bloom they were fighting and dying to sow
Seed they pitted in a briar-patch, with no glove or trowel
Grow it oak or ash or elm, bleeding arms their only flower
But fragrant, sweet as sleep perchance to dream of what might be
And in that sleep, their death, a sapling rose 'neath Tyranny
America. America. Their legacy. Our roots.
A canopy over History. A Tree that feeds on boots.
We fight for thee our reveries of Gardens with no Fall
We fertilize your Life with Death should blood not quench the Call
Our ancestors taught us all our Founding Fathers needed pen—
To sit beneath your shade may take us all our lives to win

Acknowledgments

Thanks to the editors of the *Vortex Magazine of Art and Literature*, Vol. 41, for publishing a version of "Melting."

Thanks to Jim Owen. Best schoolteacher I ever had. He began each class with the invocation: "Greetings, my wards, my lambs..." in a cigarette-soaked, bassy boom, then launched into World History as if he'd never left his postcollegiate, motorcycle tour of Europe. The view from his crowded sidecar inspired me for life, as well as many others. Rest in Peace, Shepherd. May your flock never be led to sacrificial altars.

Thanks to Heidi Ann Becker-Scripter, Eric Binnie, Wendy Blackwood, Taylor Brady, Angel Bryant, Craig Byers, Audrey T. Carroll, Énbarr Coleman, Shane Allen Curry, Jonathan Clark, Drew S. Cook, Mikayla Davis, Phillip Donaghey, Zachery Easley, Isabella Evans, Hannah Fleming, Benjamin C. Roy Cory Garrett, Jennifer Gulley, Laura Hankin, TJ Heffers, Rachel Hoge, Jake Honea, Jaime Ireland, Jesse Johnson, Kirk Jordan, Stacy Kidd, Mark Lager, Liz Larson, Briget Laskowski, Zach Long, Sandy Longhorn, Jay MacDaniel, Zach Martin, Shua Miller, Kimber Murray, Devon Norris, Jess Payne-Costaldi, LaMyia Phillips, Mel Ruth, Will Shelton, Cory Shipman, Britt Skarda, Callie Smith, Rachel Spinks, Mark Spitzer, Heather Steadham, John Vanderslice, Stephanie Vanderslice, Annika Warrick, Jack West, Keana Whale, the Arkansas Writers MFA Program and the University of Central Arkansas.

Above all, thank you, Mom.

Made in the USA
Columbia, SC
01 February 2021